A Visit to
MEXICO

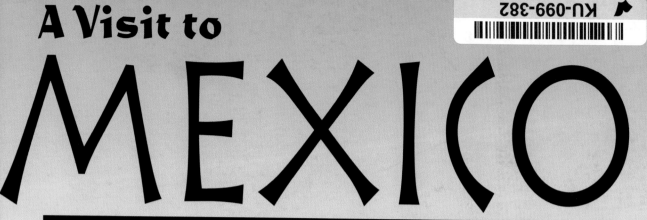

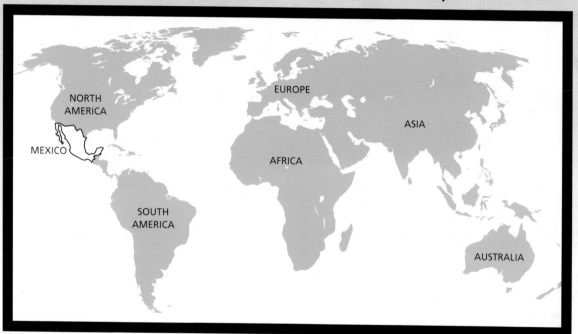

NORTH
AMERICA

EUROPE

ASIA

MEXICO

AFRICA

SOUTH
AMERICA

AUSTRALIA

Rob Alcraft

Heinemann
Schools Library and Information Services

First published in Great Britain by Heinemann Library,
Halley Court, Jordan Hill, Oxford OX2 8EJ,
a division of Reed Educational and Professional Publishing Ltd.

Heinemann is a registered trademark of Reed Educational & Professional Publishing Limited.

OXFORD MELBOURNE AUCKLAND
JOHANNESBURG BLANTYRE GABORONE
IBADAN PORTSMOUTH (NH) USA CHICAGO

Designed by AMR
Illustrations by Art Construction
Printed and bound in Hong Kong/China by South China Printing Co.

04 03 02 01 00
10 9 8 7 6 5 4 3 2 1

ISBN 0 431 08338 X

This title is also available in a hardback library edition (ISBN 0 431 08333 9).

British Library Cataloguing in Publication Data

Alcraft, Rob, 1966–
 A visit to Mexico. – (Heinemann first library)
 1. Mexico – Juvenile literature
 I.Title II.Mexico
 972

Acknowledgements
The Publishers would like to thank the following for permission to reproduce photographs:
Colourific: pp 5, 13; Hutchinson Library: p 18, Edward Parker p 7, Liba Taylor p 16; Link: Lourdes Grobet pp 15, 27, Philip Schedler p 28; Panos Pictures: Paul Smith p 8, Sean Sprague pp 10, 17, 22, 25, 26, Liba Taylor pp 12, 23; Reportage: Julio Etchart pp 19, 29; Robert Harding Picture Library: Robert Francis p 14, Robert Frerck p 20; Still Pictures p 11; Telegraph Colour Library p 6; Tony Stone Images: Demetrio Carrasco p 21; Trip: Ask Images p 9, H Sayer p 24.

Cover photograph reproduced with permission of Kodak Ltd/Robert Harding Picture Library.

Every effort has been made to contact copyright holders of any material reproduced in this book. Any omissions will be rectified in subsequent printings if notice is given to the Publisher.

Any words appearing in bold, **like this**, are explained in the Glossary.

Contents

Mexico 4

Land 6

Landmarks 8

Homes 10

Food 12

Clothes 14

Work 16

Transport 18

Language 20

School 22

Free time 24

Celebrations 26

The Arts 28

Factfile 30

Glossary 31

Index 32

Mexico

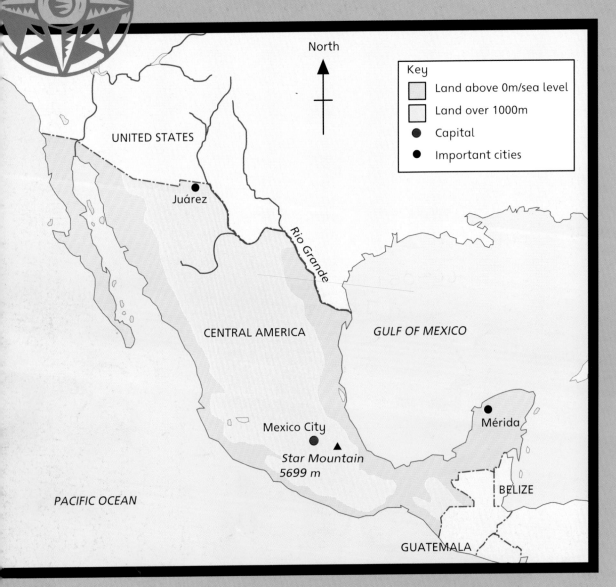

North

Key
- Land above 0m/sea level
- Land over 1000m
- ● Capital
- ● Important cities

UNITED STATES

Juárez

Rio Grande

CENTRAL AMERICA

GULF OF MEXICO

Mérida

Mexico City

Star Mountain
5699 m

PACIFIC OCEAN

BELIZE

GUATEMALA

This is a map of Mexico. Mexico is in **Central America**.

Mexico has many mountains. There are grassy **plains**, forests and long beaches. Most Mexicans live in the warm, green **highlands**.

Land

Mexico has hot deserts, where it is rocky and dry. Almost half of Mexico is desert. In some places it hardly rains at all.

High up in Mexico's mountains it can be cold. There is always snow at the top of Star Mountain. This is Mexico's highest mountain.

Landmarks

The **capital** of Mexico is called Mexico City.
It is twice as big as London. There are
19 million people living in this big, busy city.

There have been cities in Mexico for thousands of years. Here at Palenque you can see a very old **temple**. It was once part of a great city built by **Indian** people called the **Mayans**.

Homes

Most Mexican homes are small. They might have two or three rooms for a large family. Grandparents, uncles and aunts often live close by.

Homes in the countryside are like small
farms. The whole family joins in the work.
They grow **maize** and beans to eat.

Food

Mealtime is a time for the family to get together. Everyone eats pancakes called tortillas with their meal.

People in Mexico like their food hot and spicy. One treat is called guacamole, which is avocado mashed up with tomato and herbs.

Clothes

In cities Mexicans wear clothes you
would recognise. They wear jeans and
baseball caps, or cowboy hats. School
children wear smart uniforms.

In the countryside many Mexicans wear **Indian** clothes. The clothes are hand-made, and very colourful. Every part of Mexico has its own kind of Indian clothes.

Work

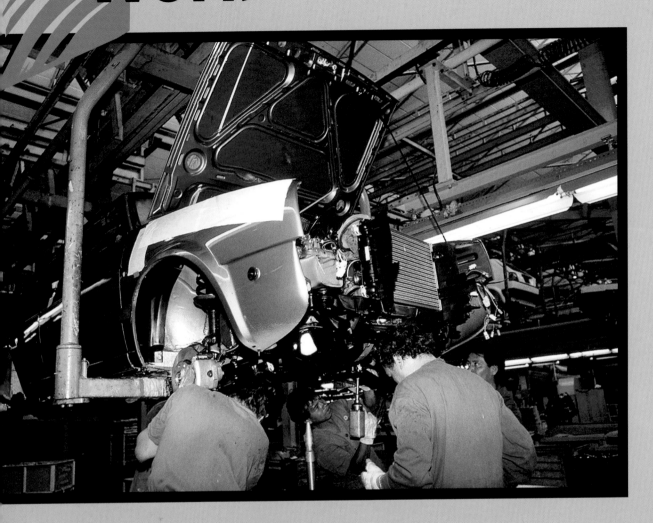

Mexican workers make cars, machinery and clothes. Other workers have jobs looking after **tourists**. They work in hotels and restaurants.

Farming is hard work. Tractors are expensive so many farmers do a lot of the work by hand or they use horses.

Transcript

Buses are the way most people travel around Mexico. They can get quite full as everyone piles their luggage on the roof and between the seats.

People use horses and donkeys to carry things along small roads. Lorries and cars carry people and loads on big roads.

Language

Mexico was once ruled by Spain, so most Mexican people speak Spanish.

Many Mexicans can speak **Indian**
languages, as well as Spanish. There
are over 50 different Indian languages
spoken in Mexico.

21

School

All young people in Mexico go to primary school from age 6 to 12. Not all children go to secondary school. Sometimes they leave to help their parents on the farm.

At school Mexican children study Spanish and maths. Country schools have vegetable gardens where children also learn about farming.

Free time

Mexicans love football and basketball. They are played everywhere. There are **bullfights** too, which big crowds come to watch.

Lots of Mexican children help out in the house in their free time. They might have animals to look after. It is work, but it can also be fun.

Celebrations

Every town and village in Mexico has its own **festival**. A band leads a parade around the streets. Everyone dresses up, and there is a party and dancing.

The Day of the Dead is the time when Mexicans remember people who are dead. Families take presents to their **relatives'** graves.

The Arts

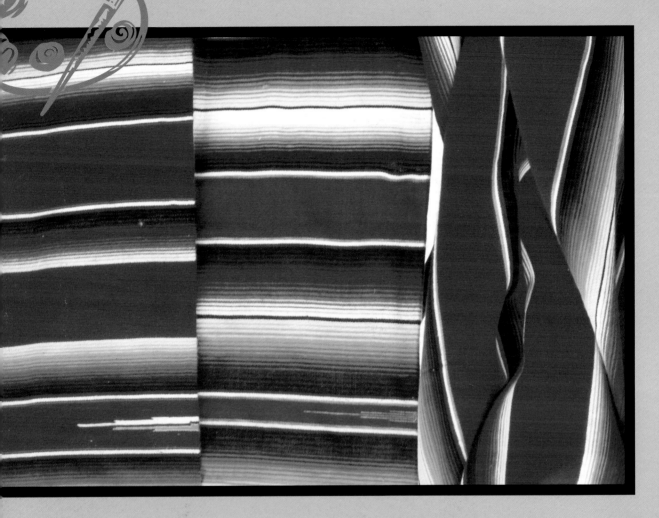

A lot of art in Mexico is made to be used, as well as looked at. People make pots, and weave cloth. They use patterns that are very, very old.

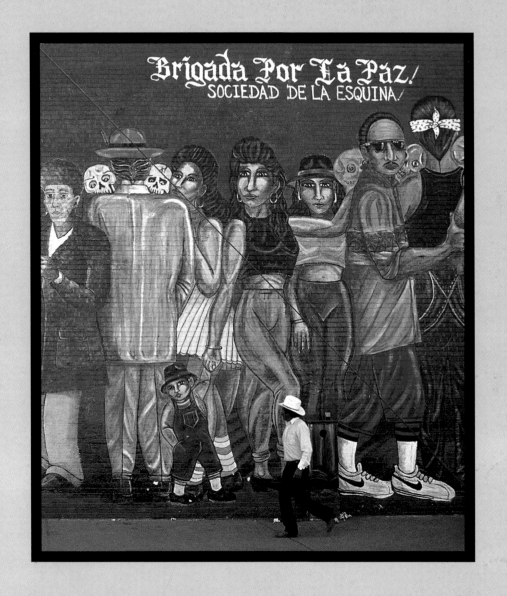

Mexican painters are famous for wall paintings, called murals. This is a mural on a street in northern Mexico.

Factfile

Name   The United States of Mexico.

Capital   The **capital** city is Mexico City.

Language   Most Mexicans speak Spanish.

Population 90 million people live in Mexico.

Money   Mexican money is called pesos.

Religion   Most Mexicans are Catholics.

Products   Mexico produces lots of coffee, cotton, silver, oil and gas, cars, tinned food and cloth.

Words you can learn

hola (o-la)	hello
adiós (ad-e-os)	goodbye
gracias (gras-e-as)	thank you
sí (see)	yes
no	no
uno (oo-no)	one
dos (doss)	two
tres	three

Glossary

bullfights   are a popular sport in Spain. A bull is put in a ring and is made angry by people with swords on horseback. At the end the bull is killed

capital   a capital city is a country's most important city. It is where the government lives

Central America   the name for all the land between Mexico and Panama

festivals   are like parties, but a whole town or country joins in

highlands   places where there are mountains

Indians   people who first lived in Mexico, before the Spanish came to rule their country

maize   looks like sweet-corn. It is made into flour and used for breads and drinks

Mayans   a people who have lived in **Central America** and Southern Mexico for over 1000 years

plains   flat places, often covered in grass and shrubs

relatives   members of your family, such as your grandparents

temple   a special place used for worship, like a church or mosque

tourists   people on holiday in a foreign country

Index

bullfighting 24, 31

cloth 28, 30

Day of the Dead 27

deserts 6

families 10, 11, 12

farming 11, 17, 22, 23

highlands 5, 31

horses 17, 19

Indian 9, 15, 21, 31

maize 11, 31

Mayans 9, 31

Mexico City 8, 30

mountains 5, 7

murals 29

snow 7

temple 9, 31